Twelve Choral Preludes
on
Gregorian Chant Themes for Organ

by JEANNE DEMESSIEUX

ISBN 0 - 87487 - 603 - 6

Summy-Birchard Inc.
exclusively distributed by
Warner Bros. Publications Inc.
15800 N.W. 48th Avenue
Miami, FL 33014

RORATE CAELI

Choral orné

I: Bourdon 8′
II: Cornet
PED: Bourdons 16′, 8′

JEANNE DEMESSIEUX

I add Flute 8′
II
I off Flute 8′

ADESTE FIDELES

Musette

I: Open Flute 8′
II: Gamba 8′, Flute 4′
PED: Bourdon 8″

II Gamba 8′, Flute 4′
I
I
II

rall. poco a poco
a tempo
II Clarinet

ATTENDE DOMINE

Choral Paraphrase

I: Foundations 8′
II: Foundations 8′, II to I
PED: Flutes 16′, 8′, I & II to Ped.

II
off I to Ped.
I
I
add I to Ped.

* A.B.: first and second motive of "Attende"

STABAT MATER

Cantabile

I: Principal 16′, Flute 8′
II: Trompette 8′
PED: Flutes 16′, 8′

II Clarinet
I
I
II Trompette 8′

II Voix celeste 16′, 8′
I Foundations 16′, 8′

VEXILLA REGIS

Prelude

I: Flutes 8′, 4′
II: Foundations 8′
PED: Foundations 16′, 8′

II off Dulciana
rit.
a tempo
I off Diapason
rit.

HOSANNA FILIO DAVID

Choral Fugue

I: Foundations 8′, 4′
II: Foundations 8′, 4′, II to I
PED: Clarion 4′

Andante ♩ = 69

poco rit.
a tempo
rit.

O FILII

Variations

I: Clarinet 8′
II: Trompette 8′
PED: Flutes 8′, 4′

I add Diap.
legato
staccato
II add Flute 2′
Ped. off Flute 4′

Meno mosso
II Flute 8′ only
Ped. soft 16′, 8′
rit.
Tempo I
legato
II Mixtures
non leg.
I
II
I
II
I
add II to Ped.

II
I
I
Foundations 8′, 4′, II to I
II add Reeds 8′, 4′
8va
II add Reeds 16′
I

(8va)
I
ff
add I to Ped.
8va
rit.
(8va)
a tempo
rit.

VENI CREATOR

Toccata

I: Full to Mixtures
II: Full to Mixtures, II to I
PED: Principals 32′, 16′, 8′, I & II to Ped.

dim.
I Foundations
cresc. poco a poco
8va

(8va)
rit.
(8va)
ff a tempo
cantus firmus
8va
rit.

UBI CARITAS

Ricercare

II: Principal 8′
PED: Flute 4′

Andante ♩ = 60

rit.

IN MANUS TUAS

Litanie

I: Voix Celeste 8′, 4′
II: Reed 8′
PED: Bourdon 8′

Andante ♩ = 100

TU ES PETRUS

Marcia

I: Tutti
II: Tutti, II to I
PED: Tutti, without heavy Reeds

Maestoso ♩ = 76

DOMINE JESU

Berceuse

I: Gamba 8′
II: Flute 8′
PED: Flute 8′

Lento ♩ = 60

II
I
add II to I 16′
add 16′
poco rit.
a tempo
off 16′
rit.
off 16′